**Gateshead** Council

Wrekenton L
Ebchester Av
Wrekenton
Gateshead
NE9 7LP

Due for Return	Due for Return	Due for Return
03/11/06		

Visit us at:
www.gateshead.gov.uk/libraries

Tel: 0191 433 8400

Newcastle Stadium

sunday, april 1st, 1973

tyneside tankard

sponsored by checkpoint

first meeting - third season

official programme 7p

HELL DRIVERS 1973

NORTH EAST MOTORSPORT

RICHARD NICHOLSON

PHOTOGRAPHY BY SPENCER OLIVER

TEMPUS

Frontispiece: Newcastle Speedway did not operate from 1971 to 1974, so Mike Parker brought stock-cars to Brough Park. Once the speedway started in 1975, however, there was never another stock-car meeting. Stock-cars and speedway bikes cannot race on the same track as the cars chew up the track and the speedway bikes need a smoother surface.

First published 2005

Tempus Publishing Limited
The Mill, Brimscombe Port,
Stroud, Gloucestershire, GL5 2QG
www.tempus-publishing.com

British Library Cataloguing in Publication Data.
A catalogue record for this book is available from the British Library.

ISBN 0 7524 3548 5

Typesetting and origination by Tempus Publishing Limited.
Printed in Great Britain.

Contents

Group of supporters gather around Maurice Robinson's bike after the meeting between Newcastle and Long Eaton on 9 May 1963.

Acknowledgements

This book would not have been possible without Spencer Oliver, who spent many years taking these photographs. I would like to thank Mrs Margaret H.S. Aisbitt for giving me the use of her father's photographs and for kindly writing about him in the introduction of this book. I would also like to thank the following people who helped to identify the photographs: Barry Wallace for help with Newcastle and Middlesbrough Speedway; Bob Boardman and Bob Ferry for their help with Sunderland Speedway; Ian Moultray for identifying the Edinburgh photographs; Mike Hunter, who has kindly allowed me to use a photograph taken at Edinburgh Speedway; and Tony Copeland for the article he wrote about Spencer for the Middlesbrough programme. Finally, I would also like to thank Ken Minns for his help with the other chapters in the book.

Introduction

This book has been produced to honour the memory of Spencer Oliver, one of the North East's best loved characters in motorcycle sport, who earned enormous respect as one of the most talented motorsports photographers this country has ever produced. Margaret H.S. Aisbitt (one of Spencer's daughters) has kindly written this piece about him for the book.

Robert Bruce Spencer Oliver was born in Walker on 24 February 1910 and died on 4 June 1984. Spencer was educated at Rutherford College in Newcastle upon Tyne and he trained as an engineer. He developed a passion for motorcars and motorcycles that fortuitously combined with his discovery of the camera. He would be seen – somewhat in the style of a Russian sea captain – at most meetings where vehicles raced, and especially at Newcastle Speedway.

Spencer cannot be properly remembered without memories of Gloria, tip-tapping behind him, always ready with a new film or the right lens and a handy pen to take notes of the rider and mark the programme in preparation for a weekly sporting article in the Chronicle *or the* Middlesbrough Gazette. *Behind the activity on the course, she burned long hours of midnight oil in the developing, printing and enlarging of photos, some of which can be enjoyed in this welcome book.*

Few people knew that Spencer was awarded a diploma of merit in the Sport photography section of the 1951 Olympics in Rome – one of a very small number in England who received such an honour.

Throughout our childhood and teenage years a vast succession of riders, ranging from novices to world champions, visited our home to share friendship engendered by a common enthusiasm for the sport. At his funeral, Walker parish church was packed with the many riders and associates who came to remember his contribution to their sport.

On behalf of my two sisters and myself, I am glad to write this foreword to a book which, together with the memorial trophy, perpetuates the memory of a most memorable man, and to thank Mr Richard Nicholson for his enthusiasm in producing this comprehensive record of Spencer's photographs.

After Spencer died, Newcastle Speedway raced for the Spencer Memorial Trophy once a season, usually in September. When Newcastle closed down, the trophy was transferred to Middlesbrough Speedway. The article below was written by Tony Copeland, the Middlesbrough promoter, and was printed in the programme on the night the trophy was presented.

The late R. Spencer Oliver was a 'big' man in every sense of the word, his imposing figure was a familiar sight at Brough Park and Cleveland Park as he went about the business of capturing for prosperity those dramatic 'once in a lifetime' moments which are the hallmark of a truly great photographer.

It was Spencer's incredible passion for motorcycle racing, coupled with his precise technical ability, which set him apart from the crowd. He could read a situation before it developed, which enabled him to capture the exact moment which lesser mortals would all too often miss.

He was a pretty good talent spotter too, singling out a young Eric Boocock as a tip for future stardom and he also prophesised that one-time failure Ivan Mauger would eventually come good if he 'got stuck in and worked hard at it'. He had an awry sense of humour and described Diamonds' Norwegian heart-throb, Dag Lovaas, as 'too bonny to be a World Champion'.

Spencer was also a big road-racing fan and did much to champion his career of the great Geordie sidecar racer Mac Dobson. Hutton Rugby's Ken Redfern was perhaps his all time favourite racer. He described Ken as the 'only true gentleman' he had ever met, and also the 'most determined rider'. Of a young Barry Sheene he was once heard to say 'that kid's got too much talent for a —— Cockney!' Spencer sadly died in 1984, and his wife Gloria, who was very much part of the team, survived him for several years but she, too, has since passed away. Spencer was the ultimate professional.

Spencer Oliver.

one

Newcastle
Speedway

Newcastle Diamonds, 1962. From left to right: Maurice Morley (co promoter), Vic Lonsdale, George Glen, Brian Craven, Gil Goldfinch, Pete Sampson, Bill Andrew, Mike Parker (promoter), Don Wilkinson (on bike).

A good action shot of Ivan Mauger, arguably one of the greatest riders to ever put on a Newcastle Diamonds race jacket. Mauger joined the Diamonds in 1963 after an unsuccessful spell in the country five years earlier.

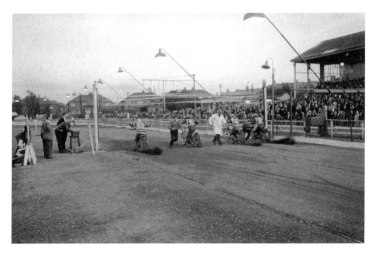

The Rider of the Night final after the match between Newcastle and Newport. From left to right: Alby Golden, Ivan Mauger, Peter Kelly and Bill Andrew. Mauger won the race (with Golden second and Kelly third) in a time of 76.25.

Ivan Mauger is presented with the Silver Sash by a Newcastle supporter. Ivan came from New Zealand in 1963 and stayed for five years, until the end of 1968. His final year with Newcastle saw him notch 23 full maximums in 36 matches and average an astonishing 11.37.

Goog Allan's fan club, who gathered on the first bend to cheer the New Zealander. Goog came over to England in 1964 to join the Diamonds. He scored 138 points in 34 matches for them that year, but the following season went on loan to Cradley Heath.

The start of heat four between Newcastle and Edinburgh in 1965. From the outside: Ken Sharples (Newcastle), Colin McKee (Edinburgh), Russ Dent (Newcastle) and Ross Nickisson (Edinburgh). Newcastle won the match 46–32.

Three of the riders called up to represent their country in the England v. Scotland test match, 31 May 1965. From left to right: Brian Craven, Nigel Boocock and Peter Kelly. England won the match 55–52. Brian rode for Liverpool, Stoke and Belle Vue before coming to Newcastle. Nigel had done most of his full-time speedway with Coventry Bees. Peter rode for Stoke, Belle Vue and Bradford until it closed, before moving to Newcastle.

NEWCASTLE
SPEEDWAY

THE DIAMONDS

British League 1965

BROUGH PARK STADIUM

NEWCASTLE-UPON-TYNE

MONDAY, 31st MAY, 1965 AT 7-30 p.m.

SECOND OFFICIAL TEST MATCH

ENGLAND
versus
SCOTLAND

Volume 5   No. 7

OFFICIAL

9D

PROGRAMME

Programme from the England *v*. Scotland second official test at Brough Park. The England team
was: N. Boocock, P. Jarman, B. Brett, P. Kelly, M. Broadbanks and C. Maidment (reserves B. Craven
and J. Kitchen). Scotland: Ken McKinlay, D. Templeton, G. Hunter, B. Scott, G. McGregor (reserves
C. McKee and B. Harkins). England won 55-52.

Newcastle riders travelling onto the track in a carriage advertising *Mary Poppins*, which was playing at the Pavilion in Newcastle at the time. Sitting with the driver are P. Kelly and B. Craven, while with their backs to him are M. Watkin, B. Brett and R. Dent. Facing them are K. Sharples and D. Gifford. Ivan Mauger is sitting on the back. The match was between Newcastle and Belle Vue and took place on 7 June 1965. Newcastle won 45-33.

Ivan Stephenson, the pit marshal at Newcastle for many years, checks to see who is riding in the next race with Stan Stevens, who was riding for Oxford in this match between Newcastle and Oxford on 13 September 1965.

Announcer Barry Wallace, talking to Peter Kelly. Peter joined Newcastle in 1963 from Stoke and played a big part in the Diamonds' Provincial League title in 1964. He continued to ride for Newcastle in the British League before moving to Berwick in Division Two.

Mrs Gloria Oliver (sitting on the right) talking to Sam Brooks and his wife Peggy. Sam was a sports reporter for many years with the *Evening Chronicle* and always covered the speedway at Brough Park.

Mike Parker, the promoter at Newcastle for many years, decides to prepare the track himself and uses the scraper to bring all the shale in from the outside of the circuit ready for the next speedway meeting.

Mike Parker watching Russ Dent warm up his bike before the meeting between Newcastle and Glasgow on 28 June 1969. Russ first appeared in the second half in 1961 and rode 6 times for the Diamonds. He became a regular in the British League side of 1965 and 1966, but requested a transfer midway through the 1967 season and joined Glasgow – he was riding for them at the time this photograph was taken.

Ole Olsen attempting to play the bagpipes at one of the supporters' social events. Arguably, Ole made a far better speedway rider than a Scottish bagpipe player…

Ole Olsen giving Bobby Moncur a ride around the track on his bike. Bobby was one of the greatest captains Newcastle United ever had and he scored a hat-trick in the 1969 Fairs Cup final.

Left: Ole Olsen sporting a race jacket that Newcastle used for only one season. Born on 16 November 1946, he was one of Denmark and Newcastle's greatest riders. Olsen joined the Diamonds in 1967, after impressing in a World Championship round. He made an immediate impact at Byker, finishing second to Ivan Mauger in the 1967 and 1968 averages, before taking over at the top in 1969 when Ivan left. In all, Ole rode in 99 matches, scoring 982 points for the Diamonds. He went on to win the world title three times after leaving Newcastle.

Below: Three World Champions together, from left to right: Anders Michanek (1974), Ole Olsen (1971, 1975 and 1978) and Ivan Mauger (1966, 1969, 1970, 1972, 1977 and 1979). All three of these great riders rode for Newcastle Diamonds.

Welcome to
NEWCASTLE
SPEEDWAY '75

Monday, March 31st,
at 7-30 p.m.
DIAMONDS
versus
TEESSIDE TIGERS
Official programme 10p

BROUGH PARK
HOME OF THE DIAMONDS

It is the dawn of a new era as Newcastle Diamonds start racing with a new promoter (Ian Thomas) and a new team. The revised line-up consisted of: T. Owen, P. Michelides, B. Havelock, T. Swales, J. Owen, R. Henderson and R. Blackadder (they were joined later in the season by T. Boyle and M. Watkin). The programme featured was for the first match of the season, a derby between Newcastle and Teesside Tigers. Newcastle won 48-30.

19

Riders who turned up for a practice day in 1975. From left to right: P. Michelides, T. Swales, R. Henderson, R. Blackadder and (on the bike) B. Havelock.

The 1976 Newcastle Diamonds, who won the league, cup and four-team tournament. From left to right: R. Blackadder, T. Owen, T. Swales, M. Watkin, J. Owen, R. Henderson, A. Cusworth, B. Havelock (on bike) and P. Michelides (kneeling).

Phil Michelides was an Australian who first tasted British speedway with the Newcastle Diamonds in 1975. He averaged 5 points a match in his first campaign, but upped that to 7.5 when he was part of the side that won the league and cup the following year. Phil suffered a dramatic loss of form in 1977, however, and quit Brough Park before the end of the season.

Bob Boardman, one of the announcers at Newcastle, invited the Surprise Sisters to come to Brough Park in March 1976. This was an all female Australian act, who had released a record called 'La booga rooga'. The single spent three weeks in the charts and reached number thirty-eight.

Nick Brightwill from Houston, Texas, performs a two-wheel drive around Brough Park on Sunday 8 October 1978. The car was an Avenger and the stunt was featured in the James Bond film *Diamonds are Forever*.

Joe Owen, riding at the height of his career for the Diamonds. He eventually left Newcastle and went to ride for Ellesmere Port. Sadly, while riding in the final match of the season at Birmingham, Joe caught the back wheel of Reg Wilson and came crashing to the ground, damaging his back. He was told that he would never walk again and would spend the rest of his life in a wheelchair.

Robbie Blackadder (left) and Ron Henderson. Robbie joined Ron Henderson and Phil Michelides as first year Aussies at Brough Park in 1975. He started from reserve to second string and eventually became a heat leader during his eight years at the club.

Tom Owen in action at Brough Park. One of the all-time great Diamonds, Tom came to the club in 1975 when Ian Thomas brought speedway back to Tyneside. He won the new National Best Pairs with Brian Havelock in the same year. Tom badly broke his leg in 1979 and sadly never recaptured his old form which led to him retiring in 1987.

Tom and Joe Owen, possibly the most famous brothers to take to a speedway track. Tom spearheaded the side as a captain and inspired the other riders in the team. Joe came with Tom to Brough Park in 1975 and went on to score an amazing 49 full maximums in 83 appearances for the 1975 to 1976 Diamonds.

Opposite above: Newcastle Diamonds, 1978. From left to right, back row: Kevin McDonald, Peter Moy, Rob Maxfield, Robbie Blackadder, Neil ('Fish') Coddington, Tom Owen. Front row: Paul Cook (mascot), Robbie Gardner, Kenny Carter, Chris Prime, David Bargh, Nigel Crabtree.

Opposite below: Tom Owen's bike after a crash. The bolt holding the front forks to the rest of the machine had snapped as he approached the first bend at around 50 mph. Tom escaped without any serious injury.

Robbie Blackadder being presented with the Julian Barnett Memorial Trophy. Julian lost his life in a road accident in 1968 whilst returning from a Newcastle away match at King's Lynn. Bob Boardman (on the left), Tom Turner (right) and another close friend, Malcolm Finley, purchased a superb trophy that they present annually to the winner of heat fifteen, the nominated riders race.

Kym Mauger and his father, Ivan Mauger. Kym joined the Newcastle Lada Diamonds in 1980. This was the first time the Newcastle speedway team had been sponsored by an individual firm.

two

Sunderland Speedway

Above: The Sunderland team, 1964. From left to right: Ken Cameron, Graham Coombes, Jim Airey, Bill Bridgett (promoter), Gordon Guasco, Ray Day, Vic Ridgeon, Dave Collins and Maury McDermott (on bike).

Left: On 21 April 1964, the first speedway meeting took place at Boldon Sunderland. The team on that historic occasion was: M. McDermott, D. Collins, S. Clark, G. Guasco, V. Ridgeon, J. Airey and R. Day.

Above: Gorden Guasco, the tall Australian, was twenty-three when he first came to Britain in order to ride for the 1964 Saints. Like his buddy, Jim Airey, he went on to represent his country in test matches. He later died in a track accident in Australia.

Below: Ken Sharples, a former Belle Vue favourite. Sharples came out of retirement to join the struggling Saints in 1964. He certainly added some backbone to the team and, after Sunderland's demise, helped Newcastle to win the Provincial League title.

SUNDERLAND
SPEEDWAY

Meeting No. 10   2nd Season

SUNDERLAND v **TEESSIDE**

(British League, Division Two)

SUNDAY JUNE 11th 1972 at 3.00 p.m.

Betting Strictly Prohibited   Official Magazine Programme 10p

A local derby between Sunderland and Teesside, 11 June 1972. Sunderland's team was: Russ Dent, George Barclay, Graeme Smith, Dave Gatenby, Jack Millen, Peter Wrathall and Jim Wells. The Teesside team was: Dave Durham, Tim Swales, Frank Affrett, Pete Reading, Roger Wright, Tony Swales and Mick Moore. The result after thirteen heats was a 39–39 draw.

Sunderland Stars team photograph, 1972. From left to right: Colin Armitstead, Jim Wells, Graeme Smith, George Barclay, Jack Millen, Dave Gatenby, Peter Wrathall and skipper Russ Dent (on machine).

The tapes go up for the meeting between Sunderland and Eastbourne, 7 May 1972. From left to right: J. Wells, R. Johns, J. Millen and G. Kennett. Sunderland lost the match 36–42.

Jack Millen, sometimes called 'Crazy Jack', hailed from New Zealand and brought a breath of fresh air to the Sunderland team. A one-off, larger-than-life character, he was the most popular rider to wear a Sunderland race jacket. He stayed with the Stars for two years and had gained 488 points in 55 matches with an average of 8.91

Opposite above: George Barclay, always known as 'Gentleman George', was born in London. A good team member who always had time for the fans, he and Terry Barclay won the Best Pairs Championship at Sunderland in 1973. George had a good club record, scoring 810 points in 120 matches with an average of 6.67.

Opposite below: George Barclay (on the extreme left) and Russ Dent making a good start. Russ joined Sunderland in 1971 and stayed right up until the end of 1974. He rode in most matches and scored the most points for Sunderland, notching up 992 in 139 matches with an average of 6.97.

Len Silver (in the light suit) with the dedicated band of St John's Ambulance crew who attended the Sunderland meeting against Crewe in May 1972.

Mike Watkin (Barrow) having a joke with Russ Dent (Sunderland) in the pits. Russ, who was from Consett, rode for Newcastle in the very first meeting to be held at the Boldon track in 1964. Seven years later, in 1971, he led the reformed Stars back into speedway. Wearing red leathers, he quickly acquired the nickname 'Captain Scarlet'.

Dave Gatenby talking to Dave Younghusband before the start of the meeting. Dave Gatenby was a local lad from Darlington who made his debut near the end of the 1971 season. He scored 479 points in 74 matches with an average of 6.24.

From left to right: George English Senior, Alan Wilmore and Bob Arnold (the starting marshal). George was a very keen supporter of speedway and was chairman of the supporters' club at Sunderland and, later, at Newcastle.

Graeme Smith, leading a race at Boldon in 1972. Graeme was born in New Zealand and had one terrific season with the Stars in 1972. Known as the 'White Knight' because of his leathers, Smith was a very good performer at Boldon, capable of beating the best in Division Two. He rode in 36 matches and scored 313 points, giving him an average of 8.29.

Peter Wrathall taking a fall on 7 July 1972. He joined Sunderland towards the end of the 1971 season from Long Eaton. A useful second-string, Pete was very popular with the fans. Midway through 1973 he felt the urge to move on again and joined Scunthorpe. He rode in 63 matches and scored 239 points, giving him a 4.27 average.

Sunderland Stars, from left to right: Ken Taylor (promoter), Peter Wrathall, Russ Dent, George Barclay, Brian Havelock, Dave Gatenby, Terry Barclay, Jim Wells, John Robson and Jack Millen (on bike).

Dave Gatenby (left) talking to Russ Dent while waiting to be introduced to the crowd. Dave joined up with the Stars in 1971 and, by 1973, his average had moved up to 7.56 – making him second only to Jack Millen. In 1974, Dave moved up to the First Division to ride for Halifax, who had seen the potential of this popular rider.

Terry Barclay, the son of Sunderland rider George Barclay, came to Sunderland to ride for the Stars in 1973. Terry, along with his father, won the best pairs that year but Terry only stayed in the team for one season, riding in 31 matches and scoring 120 points to give him an average of 4.66.

Jim Wells, who was born in Auckland, New Zealand. Wells joined the Stars in 1972 and stayed until the end of racing at Boldon. Wells improved every year and held the track record at Boldon for a while. He rode in 104 matches, scored 678 points and had an average of 6.66.

A good action shot of Brian Havelock, who was an excellent all-round motorcyclist. Havelock was born in Yarm. A late starter in speedway, Brian joined Sunderland in 1973 and captained his side the following year. He rode in 60 matches and scored 394 points, to give him an average of 6.38.

Parade line-up, from left to right: Ken Taylor, Dave Gatenby, Russ Dent, George Barclay, Jack Millen and the Ellesmere Port team.

Above: Sunderland Gladiators, 1974. From left to right: Paul Callaghan, George Barclay, Brian Havelock, Vic Harding, Jim Wells, Colin Armitstead, John Robson and Russ Dent (on bike).

Below: Paul Callaghan in action for the Gladiators. Previously with Ellesmere Port, Callaghan joined the 1974 Gladiators and, within a month, was sidelined with knee trouble. A keen but very unlucky rider as far as injuries were concerned, he only rode in four matches.

Right: Dennis Gavros lining up for the Sunderland Gladiators in 1974. Formerly a big scorer with Halifax in the 1960s, Gavros' British career was coming to a close when he came to Sunderland in 1974 to captain the Gladiators. Injuries didn't help and he announced his retirement after two–ride zero in mid-June. He rode in a total of 9 matches and scored 35 points.

Below: An action shot of Tim Swales, the Hutton Rudby Garage proprietor who joined Sunderland in 1974. He later rode for Newcastle (1975-76) before quitting the sport as a rider.

Andy Meldrum in action, 1974. Like Tim Swales, Andy was signed in June 1974. He made his home debut against Crewe, scoring 5 points.

A good action shot of Vic Harding – a likeable lad who found it very hard going in 1974, but managed 25 matches that season. He also had a brief spell with Weymouth before he was sadly killed in a track accident at Hackney.

SUNDERLAND

SPEEDWAY

GLADIATORS 1974

FRIDAY, 13th SEPTEMBER, 1974   7-30 p.m.

BRITISH LEAGUE DIVISION 2

SUNDERLAND

versus

STOKE

4th Season
Meeting No. 24

10p

This programme was from the last speedway meeting held at Boldon. The Sunderland team are listed as: J. Wells, V. Harding, B. Havelock, T. Swales, R. Dent (captain), J. Robson and John Bower. Their opponents in the Stoke team were: M. Broadbanks, B. Woodward, G. Pusey, S. Holden, A. Bridgett, A. Cusworth and S. Bastable.

Sunderland Speedway

Promoters: E.A.O. Taylor. A.K.J. Taylor

SUNDERLAND STADIUM BOLDON Co. DURHAM

Tel. No. Bolden 7250 (Race Day only) Camptown 244

OFFICIALS

Clerk of tne Course	K. Taylor	Machine Examiner
Timekeeper		Pits Marshall
Announcer	} B. Wallace	
Medical Officer (in attendance)		Team Manager
		Visiting Team Manager
Starting Marshall	G. R. Arnold	
A.C.U. Permit No. ST 452		Track Maintenance
A.C.U. Referee	R.G. Owen	Licence No. 74/15

} D. Richardson

Colin Armitstead
Chris Van Straaten

H. Harwood

St. John Ambulance Brigade in attendance
Held under the Regulations of the Speedway Control Board.

Track length 310 yards.

Track Record 4 Laps 63.2 John Hart 23.8.74
            3 Laps 48.0 John Hart 23.8.74

Barry's Bit. . .

At last, at the 67th attempt spread over four seasons of racing, Sunderland have won an away league match ! Success came at the most unlikely time, right at the end of a four-matches-in-five days spell. As the extreme points of the journey were as far apart as Workington and Weymouth it was an amazing achievement in view of the hundreds of miles of travelling involved. I wonder, too, if any other team has shrugged off a home defeat and an away trouncing of the magnitude of 60-17 in successive days to come roaring back to an away victory, let alone their first, the very next night.

Trailing by 11 points after seven heats, recovering well but still needing a last heat 5-1 for that elusive win, the saga, seemingly straight out of a schoolboy's comic, had a happy ending when Jim, who blasted away right from the start, was eventually followed over the line by Tim.

1974 at Sunderland has been a rare old season, has it not ! ? Full of promise at the outset with a new promotion and new riders, we've battled through the problems of changes in management and poor results which almost inevitably bring in small crowds, to the stage where, with everybody pulling their weight to help one another out on the track and behind the scenes, we've got what seems to me to be a settled and therefore happy set-up.

At the final reckoning Jim Wells has come out on top of the averages thanks to his brilliance of the last six weeks. Brian Havelock has rattled up nearly 300 points in league and cup matches to finish with an average of over seven points which I forecast for him in my first programme column of the season. Like Jim, Russ Dent ends up with almost identical figures to those of 1973, — a great rider for Sunderland throughout the years.

Since Tim Swales signed for the 'Gladiators' we have won seven matches. Before his arrival Sunderland had won but three out of eighteen. The figures tell the story because Tim's part in all seven successes has been considerable. Had he been with us from the start matches which were lost would have been won.

Before the season started George Barclay suggested to a young Londoner by name of Vic Harding that he should do a 'Dick Whittington' in reverse and seek his fame and fortune in the North-East. Vic, who has been living and working here since April, is now producing the form we've been waiting for.

John Robson and Brian Johnson have both benefited considerably from regular rides this year with Brian having an average of 4 points per match while John will be all out tonight against Stoke to add to the good returns of his last two home appearances. Let's see then if we can round-off '74 with a win over popular Mike Broadbanks and his team this evening.

But what of 1975 ? Three rumours are currently circulating: (a) Sunderland will not operate next year, (b) There will be racing here next year, and (c) Sunderland will transfer to Brough Park and race as Newcastle in 1975.

Rumours, — that's all they are at the moment, but two out of the three suggest we will have speedway in this particular corner of the North-East next year. If so, no doubt I'll see you there. 'Bye for now.

Barry Wallace's last column in the final Sunderland programme. The third rumour he talks about was the one that proved to be true.

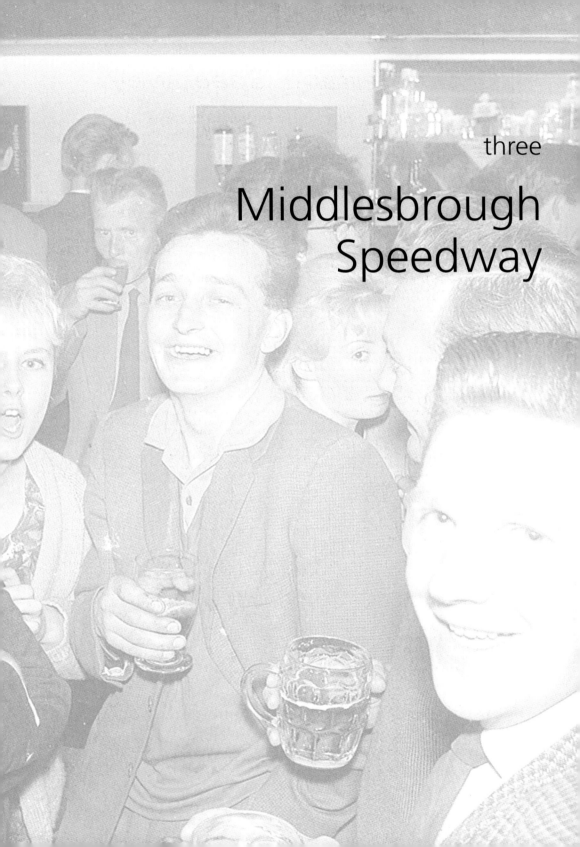

three

Middlesbrough Speedway

Above: Middlesbrough Bears, 1962. From left to right: Clive Hitch, Dave Younghusband, Freddie Greenwell, Johnnie Fitzpatrick, Eric Boothroyd, Eric Boocock and Kevin Torpie.

Below: Middlesbrough Bears, 1963. From left to right: Dave Younghusband, Clive Hitch, Freddie Greenwell, Reg Fearman (promoter), Kevin Torpie, Eric Boocock, Allan Butterfield and Bluey Scott (on bike).

Above: Allan Butterfield (left) and Dave Younghusband. Allan is a local lad, born in County Durham, who left Middlesbrough to join Newcastle Diamonds at the end of the 1964 season. His career was ended by a crash at Brough Park in May 1969, in which he sustained a severe leg injury

Right: Middlesbrough Bears *v.* Sheffield Tigers, 4 April 1963. The Middlesbrough team were: E. Boothroyd, E. Boocock, J. Fitzpatrick, C. Hitch, B. McKeown, D. Younghusband and K. Topie. Sheffield's team was comprised of: J. Dews, C. Featherby, G. Allott, T. Roper, V. Lonsdale and A. Jay. Middlesbrough lost 38-39 (both Middlesbrough riders were excluded in heat two – hence the strange result).

MIDDLESBROUGH
SPEEDWAY

CLEVELAND PARK STADIUM – "The Home of the Bears"

Coronation Street Trophy presented by KENNETH COPE

MIDDLESBROUGH "BEARS" 1962

1st MEETING — 3rd SEASON

NORTHERN LEAGUE MATCH

Middlesbrough v.
Sheffield 'Tigers'

Thursday, 4th April, 1963 at 7.30 p.m.

BETTING STRICTLY PROHIBITED

Official Programme

6 D.

Above: At the Middlesbrough *v.* Sheffield match on 4 April, star of screen and television Kenneth Cope was amongst the supporters and presented the Coronation Street Trophy to Eric Boothroyd. Kenneth, of course, is known to millions of ITV viewers as Jed Stone in *Coronation Street*.

Below: Eric Boocock standing with some Middlesbrough supporters in 1963. Eric is the younger brother of former Coventry and England international, Nigel Boocock. He had his first Middlesbrough outing in 1961 in the latter part of the season and it was immediately obvious that he was a star in the making.

Above: A scene from the Middlesbrough Christmas dinner-dance: Eric Boocock is in the black suit on the left and Allan Butterfield is in the centre, laughing at the camera.

Right: Trevor Redmond having a joke with Eric Boothroyd. Eric joined Middlesbrough in 1961 and was one of the stars of the Provincial League. Always immaculately turned out, he was in front so often that his leathers didn't get dirty! Eric promoted at Cleveland Park after retiring as a rider.

Above: Middlesbrough *v.* Cradley Heath, 6 June 1963. The riders are standing on parade, ready for the introductions to be made by Reg Fearman.

Right: Brian McKeown, formerly with Southampton, originally came from New Zealand and joined Middlesbrough in 1962. His tearaway style quickly made him a crowd favourite and he consistently hit big scores. Brian notched 310 points in his first season back after several years' absence, but a fractured leg in June 1963 brought an end to his Bears career.

Opposite above: Dave Younghusband was a discovery from the 1961 winter training school run by ex-Bear Don Wilkinson. County Durham born Younghusband made his Middlesbrough debut in 1962 and went on to ride for Halifax after Middlesbrough closed. A terrific professional, he always sported spotless machinery and leathers.

Opposite below: A sunny Thursday evening and at 7.30 p.m. the parade of riders and staff walk onto the centre green for the introduction of the teams to the crowd.

Middlesbrough Speedway

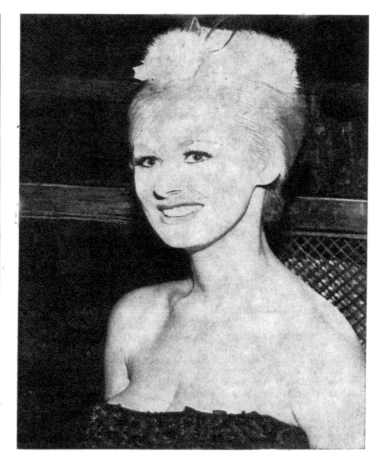

Middlesbrough v. Newport

Provincial League Match – Thursday, 16th July, 1964 at 7.30 p.m.

plus Sabrina Trophy & Grand Firework Display

Grand Gala Night Programme — One Shilling

Middlesbrough *v.* Newport in the Sabrina Trophy. Sabrina, whose real name is Norma Sykes, was born in Manchester before the war. She began her career as a cover girl and early TV appearances followed as she appeared in *Look before you Laugh* with Arthur Askey and *Ramsbottom Rides Again*. She later took part in *Blue Murder at St Trinian's* with Sid James and Frankie Vaughan.

Sabrina meeting the riders. She later presented Ivan Mauger with the Sabrina Trophy after he won the final race of the evening.

A good action shot of Clive Hitch. Clive joined the Bears in 1961 from Rayleigh. A real action man, his dives inside on the bends were something to behold and most off-putting for many an opponent.

Middlesbrough's track hours before the match was due to start. After spending time pumping the water off the surface, the meeting went ahead with just a few puddles remaining.

Peter Craven (Norwich guest), Ivan Mauger (Middlesbrough guest), Clive Hitch and Johnnie Fitzpatrick at Cleveland Park on Friday 6 September 1963. Two weeks later, Craven lost his life in a crash at Edinburgh.

MIDDLESBROUGH SPEEDWAY

CLEVELAND PARK STADIUM

2nd MEETING — 5th SEASON

World Championship
(Round 1)

Sponsored by the SUNDAY MIRROR

Thursday, 13th May, 1965 at 7-30 p.m.

BETTING STRICTLY PROHIBITED

Official Programme

9ᴰ.

The programme from a World Championship round held on 13 May 1965. The riders that took part were: M. Keen, B. Landells, B. Harkins, V. White, H. Booton, H. Bastable, G. Allan, G. Hughes, R. Day, B. Ovendon, R. Dent, J. Yacoby, I. Hughes, P. Sampson, B. Kingston and G. Coombes. At the end of the night, R. Dent was runner-up to G. Allan, who won with 15 points.

Ove Fundin presenting the Grand Easter Trophy to George Hunter on 11 April 1965. Ove rode a demonstration ride of four laps at the interval in a time of 68.25 seconds. George started riding in 1968 at Motherwell then joined Edinburgh, Coatbridge, Newcastle, Wolverhampton, Berwick and Glasgow, before moving back to Edinburgh for his final season in 1983.

Middlesbrough Bears, 1966. From left to right: E. Boothroyd (promotor), Kevin Torpie, Bill Landells, Ray Day (on bike), Vic Lonsdale, Peter Thompson, Alan Jay and Dave Gifford.

Ray Day was the top points scorer and captain of Bradford in 1960 – his first full season of racing. Yorkshireman Day was associated with many Northern tracks and is shown here in 1966 wearing Middlesbrough colours.

Ivor Brown guesting for Middlesbrough, He started his career in the Provincial League with Yarmouth. Ivor joined Cradley Heath (Heathens) at the start of the 1961 season. A hard rider, Ivor had a bit of a tough reputation.

Left: Tom Leadbitter was born at Lichfield and joined Teesside for their British League Division Two debut season in 1968. He topped the Tigers' averages in 1970 and went into Division One with Leicester and then Wolverhampton for the next four years. Tom rejoined Teesside in 1975 and topped the averages again on 9.40.

Below: The Teesside team, from left to right: Tim Swales, Pete Reading, Dave Durham, John Spilsbury, Terry Lee and Bruce Forrester.

Above: Tim Swales and Pete Reading. Retford-born Pete was a member of Teesside's 1968 team for the start of British League Division Two. He rode for the club in every year until 1980, when he made his last appearance.

Below: Teesside Tigers, from left to right: Pete Reading, Frank Auffret, Dave Durham, Bruce Forrester (on bike), Mick Moore, Tim Swales, Henry Atkinson (team manager) and Tony Swales.

Opposite: A local derby between Teesside and Newcastle. Riding for Teesside were: S. Wilcock, M. Dixon, P. Smith, N. Close, M. Cusworth, P. Spink and B. Watts. Newcastle comprised: T. Owen, G. Stapleton, R. Blackadder, K. Carter, R. Gardner, N. Coddington and R. Hunter. Newcastle won the match 42–36.

Left: Dave Durham, who was born in Wakefield, made his debut for Teesside in 1968, the first year of British League Division Two. His best season was 1972, when he scored 316 points in 36 matches. Dave remained a one-club man and retired in 1975.

Below: Tim Swales (number 5) and Bruce Forrester (number 1) in Teesside colours during 1972. Bruce, who was born in Leicester, joined the Teesside Tigers in 1969 and made 167 appearances. He topped the Tigers' averages in 1971 and 1973, and was on 8.91 in 1975 when off-track business pressures forced him to seek a move to a Sunday track.

ST Teesside Speedway

11th Season

TEESSIDE
TIGERS
V
NEWCASTLE

NATIONAL LEAGUE MATCH

THURSDAY, 21st SEPTEMBER, 1978

N⁰ 456

Official Programme **15p**

Above: An action photograph of Alan Emerson in 1976. Alan, who was born at Haltwhistle, made his Teesside debut as a sixteen-year-old in 1973. A big favourite through his style of attacking the bends, Emerson topped the club averages in 1976 and 1977. He later rode for Workington and arch-rivals Newcastle.

Below: Pete Smith, who was born in Barnsley, made his debut for Teesside in 1975 and was a heat leader by the end of 1978. After a spell with King's Lynn, Leicester and Stoke, Smith had one final year with Middlesbrough in 1984.

Above: Ron Henderson (Newcastle) leads Tom Leadbitter (Teesside) in a local derby match at Brough Park.

Right: Nigel Close was born at Bowes (County Durham) and is the son of former Newcastle rider Derek Close. Nigel made his Teesside debut in 1976. He joined Berwick in 1979 before moving again, this time to Glasgow.

An action photograph of Pete Reading. He amassed a total of 371 matches for the Tigers and scored 2199.5 points – a magnificent effort.

Workington's Andy Margarson (on the right) fighting for second place with Steve Wilcock. Steve was born in Dewsbury and rode for Bradford in 1974 and 1975 before starting a long and brilliant association with Middlesbrough in 1976. He topped 400 points in a season five times and scored over 300 in four other years with the club.

four

Silloth
Airfield

G. Buchan (number 47), on a Norton, in the final race at Silloth, 26 July 1964. He leads second placed D. Padgett, on a Yamaha, with S.T. Smith on an MV in third place. George Buchan was Scottish Champion for many years.

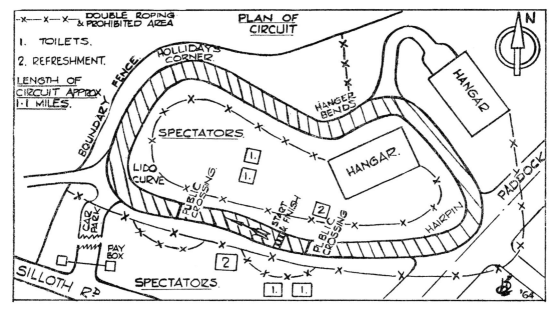

Silloth as it was in 1963, showing all areas of the circuit. Silloth Airfield was opened in 1939 to meet the demands of the Royal Air Force. After the war, it was not used until 1960, when race meetings were introduced on a regular basis.

NORTH EAST
MOTOR CYCLE
RACING CLUB

presents

The first time ever in Cumberland

Motor Cycle
Road Racing

Silloth Airfield,
Cumberland

Sunday, 26th July, 1964

First Race 1 p.m.

OFFICIAL PROGRAMME 1/-

A programme from one of the meetings at the Cumberland track in 1966, with nine races for solo bikes from 50cc up to 500cc and three events with unlimited sidecars. The top five finishers went through to a grand final.

D.G. Harrison (number 18) of Newcastle, taking a corner at speed on a 250cc Aermacchi. This bike was produced in a factory on the shores of Lake Varese. In 1960 the company merged with Harley-Davidson to produce a 250cc motorbike.

J. Learmouth (number 83) of Penicuik, cornering on a 250cc Honda. This was one of the early bikes produced by the Japanese company for racing. In 1963 Honda decided to halt the production of road bikes so that they could concentrate on Formula One.

A. Whittaker (Wakefield), riding a 250cc Greeves. The Greeves was produced by a small English motorcycle company, founded by Bert Greeves, that made lightweight two-stroke road bikes.

C. Ward (Rothwell), riding a 350cc Norton and leading W. Rae (Wakefield) on a 350cc AJS, followed closely by D. Padgett (Batley) on a Yamaha. A.J. Stevens & Co. Ltd started to make the first AJS engines in 1909. In 1913, the AJS factory introduced a motorcycle with a sidecar.

The riders line up for the final race. They are B. Robertson (number 20, Alnwick), B. Winter (number 91, Sunderland), T.W. Gardener (number 13, Newcastle), M.L. Hosgood (number 94, Prestatyn), R. Wilding (number 33, Hoole), S. Murray (number 38, Hoole) and T.D. Robinson (number 40, Clitheroe).

T.D. Robinson (number 40, Clitheroe) riding a Bultaco 125cc. Jesus Romero and his brother, Pedro, started the company that produced the Bultaco motorbike.

The final heat of the sidecars unlimited with M. Hobson (number 58, Gosforth) on a Norton leading J. Mines (number 61, Darlington) on a Triumph/Norton.

Heat three of the sidecars unlimited shows R.F. Chapman (number 63, Saxlby) on a BSA riding for a place in the final race of the day.

North East Motor Cycle Racing Club
AND
The makers of "Senior Service" Cigarettes

present

Motor Cycle
Road Racing

at

SILLOTH AIRFIELD
CUMBERLAND

Sunday, 22nd August, 1965

Official Programme   *Price 1/-*

This meeting, like all the other meetings at Silloth, was organised by the North East Motor Cycle Club, who started racing in 1964 with a membership of 250. It was clearly successful, as by 1965 membership had risen to more than 400.

M. Hobson (number 4, Newcastle) and passenger M. Burns on a Triumph/Norton, sponsored by -T. Cowie Ltd, coming out of the final corner to win the second heat of the Ariel Trophy Race.

F. Wallis (number 18, Beeston) and passenger A. Barton just keeping ahead coming out of one of the corners in the Ariel Trophy Race.

Event six was the sidecar invitation race. J.E. Fawcett (number 20, Murton) and passenger M. Kettlestring are leading F. Wallis (number 18, Beeston) and passenger A. Barton. The result of the race was: first, B. McAnelly and passenger P. Horsefield (Gateshead); second, J.E. Fawcett and passenger Kettleworth (Murton); third, M. Hobson and passenger M. Burns (Newcastle).

Action from the Senior Service Tipped Trophy Race, and A. Ratcliffe (number 88, Boldon) leads G. Stringer (number 95, Rothwell). The winner of the race was G. Buchan (Inverness) on a Norton.

The Ariel Trophy Race for three-wheelers up to 1,000cc, and R. Clark and passenger L. Bennett (Whitley Bay) lead number 2 T.W. Windle and passenger A. Haigh (Sheffield). The latter pair won the race.

The sidecar invitation race, with N. Rumsey and passenger C. Sharpe (number 28, Seaham) fighting for the lead with V.G. McFarlane and passenger J.F. Whaite (number 19, Preston). The result of the race was: first, B. McAnelly (Gateshead); second, J.E. Fawcett (Preston); third, V.G. McFarlane (Preston).

The Nelson Trophy final and D. Catterson (number 3, Paisley) is leading M.J. Pomfret (number 17, Newport). The result of the race was: first, E.A. Johnson (North Shields); second, B. Richards (Ulverston); third, A.E. Weaver (Ormskirk).

The final of the Senior Service Trophy Race, with number 143 leading from G. Buchan (Inverness), while A. Barton (Beeston) is in fourth position. The race resulted in a win for George Buchan.

The first heat of the Nelson Trophy and M. I'Anson (number 16, Newcastle) on a Honda leads from J. Poyzer (number 15, Glossop) on a Bultaco. The result of the race was: first, E.A. Johnson (North Shields) on a Honda; second, A.E. Weaver (Ormskirk) on a Honda; third, F.E. Holmes (Barrhead) on a Bultaco.

Senior Service Tipped Trophy Race second heat and A. Dugdale (number 103, Warrington) takes the corner tight with J.R. Humble (number 112, Bishop Auckland) following close behind.

SOLWAY MOTOR CYCLE RACING CLUB

present the

BENSON and HEDGES TROPHY RACES

Silloth Airfield
CUMBERLAND

Sunday, 21st August, 1966

FIRST RACE 1-0 p.m.

This event was organised by Solway Motor Cycle Racing Club, with the appointed stewards being D. Geddes and T. Nicholson. There were 180 solo competitors and 36 sidecar entrants for this meeting, which was sponsored by Hamlet cigars.

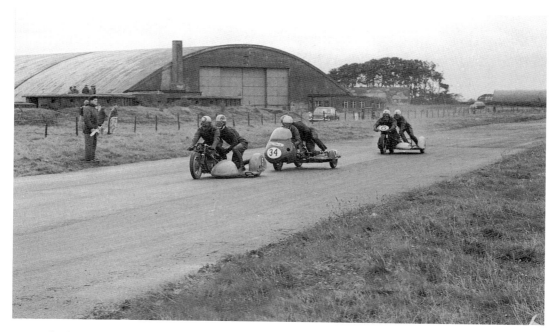

The final of the Benson & Hedges Kingsize Trophy for three-wheelers (unlimited). J. Fawcett (number 5, York) and passenger M. Kettlestring are leading from R. Green (number 34, Ireland) and passenger J. Silto, with K. Southam (number 6, Brampton) and passenger B. Chetwyn in third place.

The final of the Stirling Trophy and P. Richards (number 117, Australia), on a 500cc Norton, is leading from J. Simms (number 60, Sheffield) on a 500cc Norton.

A rider misjudges the conditions of the track and takes a tumble on one of the corners at Silloth Airfield. Track conditions on that day were poor and extra care was needed.

Action from the Benson & Hedges Kingsize three-wheelers (unlimited) race, as K. Southam (number 6, Brampton) and passenger B. Chetwyn hold the lead on one of the tight corners. They are closely followed by M. Hobson (number 1, Newcastle) and passenger G. Atkinson.

Heat two of the Benson & Hedges Kingsize Trophy race, with J. Fawcett (number 5, York) and passenger M. Kettlestring leading M. Hobson (number 1, Newcastle) and passenger G. Atkinson.

Benson & Hedges Kingsize three-wheelers (unlimited) race. M. Hodson (number 1, Newcastle) and passenger G. Atkinson were sponsored by T. Cowie Ltd. Malcolm Hobson was killed in an accident on Bray Hill in the Isle of Man in 1978, along with passenger Kenny Birch.

N. Mead (number 20, York), who was an ex-grasstrack racer, and passenger D. Reynolds on a Triumph sponsored by Slack & Reynolds, attempting to take a tight corner in the first heat of the Benson & Hedges Kingsize three-wheelers (unlimited) race.

V. McFarline (number 2, Preston) and passenger J. Whaite on a BSA, trying to overtake the race leader in the Benson & Hedges Kingsize three-wheelers (unlimited) race.

DAILY MAIL

Above: Charterhall hosted many motor racing events. Stirling Moss, Mike Hawthorn and Jim Clark were just a few of the great drivers who used the track. The track closed in 1964 when the Borders Club founded a new circuit at Ingliston.

Left: Programme from Charterhall, 1963. Racing started at 10.30 a.m. and finished at 1.00 p.m. There were ten events, including racing cars, touring cars, solo motorcycles and sidecars. The climax of the meeting was the BMRC Trophy Handicap final.

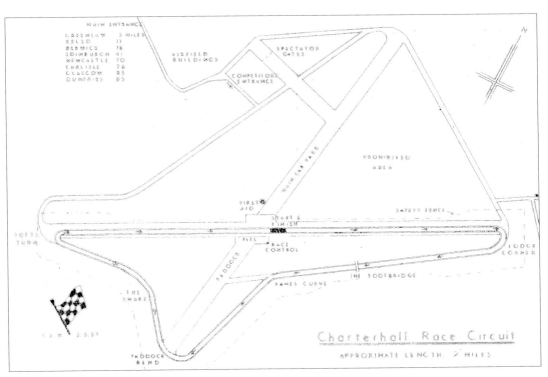

Charterhall circuit as shown in the programme. Each lap was two miles and the events varied from six to ten laps, with the final race covering twelve laps.

The winner of event six was J. Mackay in a 1,220cc Shannon-Climax. In the final of the Border Motor Racing Club Trophy Handicap final, car 29 came eleventh out of fourteen competitors.

G.A. Percival (number 21) racing a Ford Anglia 1,476cc. He came fifth out of seventeen runners. The Ford Anglia was produced in the early 1960s as a small family saloon.

The leader is A.C. Goodfellow in a 1,216cc TVR Grantura, closely followed by J.E. Milne in a 998cc Austin-Healey Sprite. There were three classes of cars in the same race: under 1,100cc, 1,000cc to 2,000cc and over 2,000cc. The first three in each class went into the final.

J.E. Milne in a 1,074cc Cooper Mini S leading the field in event five of the touring cars. G.A. Percival won the race in a 1,476cc Ford Anglia, while second was W.A. Borrowman in a 997 Austin Cooper and third was J. Bridges in a 997 Mini Cooper.

In the pits and waiting to race is Miss J. Hutchingson's 1,498cc Terrier Mk 2, behind the Morris Cooper of J.R. Calder.

J.E. Milne, in an MG Midget, passes a driver who has just skidded and turned over on the race track.

Event six of the sports cars race and G.P.D. Bellerby is racing a 998cc MG Midget. The winner was J. Mackay in a Shannon–Climax, while second was J.L. Romanes in a Lotus 23 and third E. Liddell in a Lola.

Event two of the grand touring cars race. W.A. Borrowman, in an Austin-Cooper, eventually came in ninth out of the eighteen cars that started the race.

Riders waiting on the grid for the start of the sidecars (unlimited) race. G.D. Bell (number 1, Bedlington) and passenger B. Bewley are on a Norton 500cc, and are against J. Crick (number 7, Darfield) and passenger D Senior, M. Hobson (number 6, Newcastle) and passenger J. Hartridge on a BSA 500cc. Number 7 eventually won the race. George Bell is the father of Ian and Jeff, who were winners of the sidecar event in the Isle of Man. George was also the founder member of the North East Motorcycle Racing Club.

B. McAnelly (Gateshead) and passenger G. Layfield on a Norton 500cc sidecar. These two lads came ninth out of ten runners. Tragically, both the McAnelly brothers were later killed racing sidecars.

Winner of event eight, the sidecars (unlimited) race, John Crick (Darfield) and passenger Dave Senior on a BMW/Triumph 650cc.

The fifth-placed pair in event eight, the sidecars (unlimited), were Charlie Smith (Gateshead) and passenger Jim Wilkie racing a Vincent 998cc sidecar.

The winner of event seven, solo motorcycles 201–250cc, was S. Wright (Barnsley) riding a Honda 250cc. He won the race in a time of 16 minutes and 7.04 sec, with an average speed of 74.42 mph.

Les Siddle (Shiremoor) and passenger John Barker on a BSA sidecar. This sidecar came third in event eight, the sidecars (unlimited) race.

six

Croft
Aerodrome

During the Second World War, Croft Aerodrome was used by the Canadian Bomber Squadron 419 and, after the war was finished, became unused. In 1964, local motoring organizations started to use the aerodrome for racing. To this day, they are still racing bikes and cars at the circuit.

Race three, event two of the sidecars on 13 May 1972 and R. Bell (Newcastle) and passenger G. Russell are going through the chicane in front of N. Riley (Warrington) and passenger K. Birch.

The final of the sidecars on 13 May 1972. R. Smith (Bury) and passenger C. Longbottom are going round the corner ahead of M. Croft (Lancaster) and passenger L. Batty.

Taking a break between races is A.E. Jackson, from Preston, standing behind his 350cc Yamaha. He was sponsored by J.R. Henderson Transport.

Race eight on 13 April 1974 and just behind the leader R.V. Bodden (number 44, Wrexham) is G.W. Sellars (number 10, Greatham) with J.H. Chisholm (number 32, Blyth) in fourth position.

Race three on 13 April 1974 and D. French (Bradford) and passenger J. Teal are leading from P.W. Smith (Hawick) and passenger I. Smith, with G. Laycock (Skipton) and passenger D. Seed following behind on the inside of the track.

I. Bellamy and passenger S. Davison in race four on 7 May 1974. The winner was M. White and passenger P. Oliver, while second was D. Greasley and third P. Rogers.

Race six on 18 May 1974 and E. Owen (number 32, Penrith) and passenger P. Howe, on a Triumph, are leading M. Seddon (number 4, Lancashire) and passenger M. Harrison, on a HTS, closely followed by C. Andrews (number 28, York) and passenger M. Andrews, on a Honda.

NORTH EAST MOTOR CYCLE RACING CLUB

National Road Race Meeting
Croft Autodrome Near Darlington
KEN REDFERN TROPHY

Saturday 21st September
1974 at 1.00 p.m.

Admission Charge 60p. Permit No. A.C.U. 789

A programme from Croft Autodrome (as it is now called). It shows the Ken Redfern Trophy, which is raced every year around about September in memory of the rider, who was killed in a road accident on 30 June 1973.

KEN REDFERN

The primary object of this meeting today is to honour the memory of KEN REDFERN a North East Motorcycle Racing Club member who rose from the ranks of ordinary Clubmen to become one of the established stars in National and International road racing before he met his death in a road accident on Saturday the 30th June 1973.

Ken's rise to fame was achieved in an incredibly short space of time with his first taste of real success coming in 1969 when he finished second to Giacomo Agostini at Cadwell and again at Mallory beating the best in the land to do so.

These two achievements, the first of many to follow, brought him into sharp focus as a potential International Star of the future if ever there was one and it was not long after this that the promise he had evinced was fully realised with a series of wins and record laps second to none at all the major short circuits throughout the country.

At Croft, apart from his numerous wins, he established on the 2nd of May 1970 an 'Overall' two wheeler lap record at an average speed of 81.4 mph time 1m 17.4s. This record was accomplished on a 750cc Norton Domiracer and remained unbroken until the 29th of September 1973 although it was equalled on the 27th of August 1973.

Other lap records established by Ken at Croft were in the 350cc category in which on the 1st of May 1971 on a 350 Yamsel he raised the existing lap record held by the late Steve Machin to 79.95 mph, time 1m 18.8s which stood until the 6th of May 1972 when Ken again raised the 350cc lap record to 80.36 mph time 1m 18.4s to become the first to break the 80 mph barrier on a 350cc machine at Croft. All these achievements were accomplished in Middlesbrough and District Motor Club National Events.

Abroad he competed successfully in Sweden, France and British Guiana especially Guiana where by his personal charm, politeness and artistry made him a celebrity overnight to a degree seldom achieved by anyone in the world of sport.

The true measure of the kind of man Ken was was adequately summed up in an anecdote told to me by his contemporary Mick Grant as follows:- Ken and Mick were having a real dice for first place, with Mick at the time leading. Ken took Mick on a corner then slowed down and waved Mick on only to pass him again and win. After the race Mick asked Ken why he had slowed down and waved him on, Ken's reply was simple and sincere and it was he thought he had been a bit naughty by passing Mick the way he did on the corner and apologised for any consternation he may have caused Mick at the time. Mick could hardly believe his ears as he considered, rightly, that Ken had passed him fairly and squarely on the first occasion. Mick's comment at the time was that Ken could pass anybody at anytime on his day regardless of who they were. Nevertheless Mick considered Ken's chivalrous and Gentlemanly conduct on and off the track to be out of this world in this day and age and admired Ken all the more for it.

In conclusion I would like to say that in my association with motorsport in general, stretching back over half a century, I have seldom met anyone more fitted to the title of 'Gentleman' than Ken Redfern and for those who knew him his passing has left a void which will never be filled.

SPENCER OLIVER

The article that appeared in the programme each year (written by Spencer Oliver) about Ken Redfern.

After the Laird of Croft Championship final round on 28 September 1974, Roger Marshall (British Solo Champion) presents the winner, Phil Gurneron, who was on a Yamaha. In second place was Roger Nott, also on a Yamaha, and in third David Green, riding a Maxton.

Race nine on 28 September 1974 and Roy Swanwick (number 55), riding a Norton 750cc, is closely followed by Mick Harrison (number 52) on an Aermacchi 350cc. The winner of the race was Roger Nott. Brian Peters was second and Jeff March in third place.

Event three, heat one on 5 October 1974 and I. MacCallum and passenger R. Raine are racing an Imp 875. This meeting was organised by Cheshire Motor Cycle Road Racing Club.

Race two of the sidecars and Bruce Cartwright (Knaresborough) and passenger M. Staiano are racing a Tri-Star 649cc.

Taking the chicane in race five of event one on 3 May 1975 and A. Jackson (Kendal) is on a Crooks Suzuki 249cc.

Opposite above: Action from the fourth round of the Club Championship on 8 May 1975. David Jeff is leading on a Kawasaki 500cc. Just behind him is Kenneth Harmer on a Commando 830cc and in third place is Harry Plews on a Kawasaki 500cc. The winner of the race was Alan Davies on a Trident 750cc.

Opposite below: The 1976 British Solo Championship was held on 19 June 1976. Mike Dowkes (Scarborough) is racing a Norton and was sponsored by Dowsons Motorcycles of Scarborough.

The final of the First Round New Era Championship covered five laps of the course. Mark Middleton on a Yamaha 700cc is closely followed on the outside by Leslie Rushworth on a Laverda 1,000cc. Behind them is Donald Hill (number 7) on a Commando 750cc, while trailing at the back is Alan Jackson (number 119) on a Silk 700cc.

Sidecars racing for the Ken Blacklock Trophy on 17 September 1977. Taking a short lead are Russ Leek (Lancaster) and passenger M. Cowan. They eventually came third in this race, which was the first of two heats.

CROFT autodrome

B.A.R.C. Championships Race Meeting

Sunday 5th AUGUST 1979

For conditions of admission, see inside,

OFFICIAL PROGRAMME 20p

The programme from a British Automobile Racing Club event staged on 5 August 1979. The meeting included modified sports cars, Formula Ford 1600 cars, production saloons, clubman sports, Formule Libre and special saloons.

Event one of the modified sports cars class 'B' on 5 August 1979 and Jon Fletcher is racing a Lotus Elan 1800cc.

Event seven of the Formule Libre class 'A' race on 5 August 1979 and George McMillen (North Berwick) is racing a Chevron B55 (Swindon).

Racing in one of the main events in August 1979, Kevin McCormick is using a Mallock Mk 20B.

The British Automobile Racing Club Championship was held on 23 September 1979. Nicky Ellis (Newcastle upon Tyne) is racing an Elan that has been sponsored by Cowgate Motor Company.

The crowd watch as competitor number 3, W.A. Robson, waits to start the touring car race in his Saab 841cc. The course was exactly a quarter of a mile in length and cars travelled at speeds of more than seventy miles per hour over the finishing line.

Messrs Gallaher presenting one of the competitors with the Senior Service Silver casket for the fastest time of the day at the Wallsend Sprint, 10 May 1964.

A. Barton (number 31) trying to beat the fastest time in the Wallsend Sprint, 10 May 1964. He was driving a Morris 1,000 and represented the Newcastle & District Motor Club.

Crowds waiting for the Wallsend Sprint to start, 10 May 1963.

Motor bikes and sidecars racing across the grass at Marsden South Shields was a common sight in the 1960s. This photograph was taken in May 1968 and shows a large crowd watching Jim and Peter Anderson on an all-welded special completing another lap.

Another scene at Marsden, South Shields in May 1968, showing the scrambling bikes just starting a race. This part of the North East was a popular place for competitors to try their luck over the uneven surface of the grass.

Bents Park, South Shields, 30 June 1968. Ted Scott and passenger Allan Blewitt both won future grass-track championships driving their own outfits.

Keith Nesbitt taking a tight corner in the scrambling event at Shortly Spa on 3 May 1968. The motorbikes were very heavy to handle and it took great skill to complete the course.

Allan Butterfield, seen at Bollihope Common in June 1968 with his son, John. Allan was a keen trials rider, but is better known as a speedway rider. A County Durham lad, he joined Newcastle from Middlesbrough and made 100 British League appearances for the Diamonds between 1965 and 1969.

Competitors awaiting the start of the trials competition at Bollihope Common, June 1968.

Attempting a difficult part of the course at Bollihope Common, June 1968. Competitors had to complete a set course over rocks, water and hill climbs, without putting their feet on the ground, to reach the end of the course.

Annfield Plain, Durham on 21 June 1968 and Dave Winfield is seen here trying to complete a tricky course, made even more difficult after heavy rain had rendered it very muddy.

Annfield Plain, Durham on 21 June 1968 and Ken Minns and George Facey get into trouble in the adverse conditions.

Hagg House Farm, Ellington on 9 June 1968 and Jeff Willson, the driver of the outfit, is completing the course with a very good time.

Competitors racing over the scrambling course at Shilbottle in May 1968. Other events also took place that day.

Dave Younghusband was a keen trials rider, but is better known for speedway. Born in County Durham he rode for Newcastle, Middlesbrough and Halifax before becoming team manager for Newcastle Diamonds.

Seaton Delaval in 1969 and riders are getting ready to start the tricky trials course.

Mike Watkin attempting the trials course at Seaton Delaval in 1969. Mike is better known for his speedway and rode for Newcastle Diamonds between 1971 and 1974. He resumed with the promotion in 1975, before a crash at Workington resulted in his retirement from the sport.

Starting young at Iveston on 10 June 1969: two children with their own sidecar are practising for when they get old enough to follow in their father's footsteps.

Iveston on 10 June 1969 and one of the competitors gets ready as the spectators make their way to the course.

Dave Winfield clearing one of the jumps at Iveston on 10 June 1969. Dave was the top North East rider and owner of Mile End Motors in South Shields.

Bebside on 24 August 1969 and A. Brown (Pittenween) is on a 500cc Jap speedway bike. He won his heat and went on to win the final.

Again at Bebside on 24 August 1969. The riders, from left to right, are: J. Nesbitt (number 63, Eyemouth), T. Ray (number 82, Duns), M. Knott (number 8, Wallsend) and E. Wells (number 103, Catterick Camp).

Bebside, 24 August 1969 and A. Waugh is pictured on a 250cc CZ. He came in third in the heat and won the final of the day.

Ken Minns (Durham) on a 500cc Rastus at Bebside on 24 August 1969. He was unbeaten on the day, winning all three races he entered. Ken now has a garage in Pity Me called Merlin Coachworks and produces sidecars to order.

Opposite above: J. Barrie from Wooler racing a 500cc Metisse at Bebside, 24 August 1969.

Opposite below: Riders line up for the start of the final race at Bebside on 24 August 1969. They are: J. Nesbitt (number 63, Eyemouth), M. Knott (number 8, Wallsend), B.A. Brown (number 54, Pittenneen), G. Thompson (number 24, Blaydon), J. Barrie (number 89, Wooler), D. Fairless (number 9, Newcastle) and B. Stuart (number 293, Duns).

Other titles published by Tempus

Durham CCC: 100 Greats

MATTHEW APPLEBY

Durham, the youngest first-class county, has a record as proud as any other. Since the club's elevation to the top rank in 1992 Test stars including Ian Botham, Dean Jones and David Boon have attracted loyal and knowledgeable crowds, and more recently the county has produced home-grown stars like England international players Steve Harmison and Paul Collingwood. With illustrations, biographies and statistics of Durham CCC's finest cricketers, this book pays tribute to the men who are the county's cricketing history.

0 7524 3195 1

Hot Rod Racing: The Golden Years

RICHARD JOHN NEIL

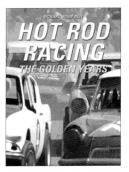

The 1970s saw hot rod racing at the height of its popularity, with large crowds flocking to watch their heroes in action every week. Developed in the mid-1960s as a 'purer' alternative to the 'crash and bash' of stock car racing, this non-contact form of racing flourished in the 1970s to the point where a World Championship and an international Test series were contested. Here, in over 200 photographs, are the cars, the drivers, the circuits and the events from those golden years of racing.

0 7524 3241 9

Hull Speedway 1930-81

ROGER HULBERT

The first instalment of a two-volume history of speedway in the city, *Hull Speedway 1930-81* brings to life the intriguing heritage of this club, recording its ups and downs over the first five decades of its existence. The team has performed at the top level of British speedway and has been represented by greats like Ivan Mauger, Barry Briggs and Sam Ermolenko. It includes comprehensive statistical information and many rare pictures, and a second volume, *Hull Speedway: Craven Park, The First Ten Years* brings the story up to date.

0 7524 3200 1

Fighting Men of the North

RONNIE WHARTON

The North East of England has been witness to some of the finest fighting men in the world. Featured here are twenty-two of the greatest over the past 100 years, with full biographies and career statistics. Beginning with the likes of Will Curley, George Chrisp and Jack Palmer, *Fighting Men of the North* tells the stories of the region's great glove champions right up to present-day fighters Cornelius Carr and Michael Hunter. It recalls times when boxing venues in the North East were as plentiful as picture houses and is an essential read for any fan of British boxing.

0 7524 3551 5

If you are interested in purchasing other books published by Tempus, or in case you have difficulty finding any Tempus books in your local bookshop, you can also place orders directly through our website

www.tempus-publishing.com